2ⁿᵈ Edition

PROVEN MARKETING STRATEGIES
for
Conflict Resolutionists
A Hands-On Workbook

Natalie J. Armstrong-Motin

"The best way to predict the future is to create it."
– Peter Drucker

Marketing as a Mindset

Marketing is a mindset and an attitude as much as it is an activity. It pervades every aspect of every interaction with every potential or current client. Many professional service providers think of cheesy, misleading, or even fraudulent advertising when they think of marketing. Frequently the picture that comes to mind when marketing is mentioned is the ever-lasting image of a car salesman. We tend to have an instant distrust of people who are trying to sell us something. Distrust in the resolution industry or its providers can be death to both the industry and individuals. Trust is one of our strongest commodities.

Marketing to potential clients without raising the red flag of mistrust can be accomplished in myriad ways. First it's important to understand that marketing your practice should be very intentional. Intentionally marketing your practice can be done either "apparently" or "inconspicuously" or a combination of these two states. Apparent methods of marketing can be speaking publicly, publishing an article, distributing business cards and brochures, leading prospects to a web site or blogging. However, every time you answer the phone, respond to correspondence, talk about your industry or practice at a social event or with your neighbor over the fence – you are marketing. Often, it is these softer methods of marketing that are more effective.

Many practitioners don't even consider that their physical appearance may have an impact on the hearing outcome as well as have an impact on whether or not they receive any repeat business. Now I'm not suggesting that unless you look like an Elle McPherson or George Clooney you'll fail, what I am suggesting is that marketing a successful practice requires a complete awareness of the perception your clients and potential clients have of you during every single interaction. Presenting yourself and your practice in the most professional manner isn't just good marketing – it's good business. Remember, that when you present print or internet collateral to potential clients, that collateral is speaking on your behalf in lieu of a personal meeting. Is it imbued with the professional image you and clients are looking for? What will be your target market's perception?

Promoting your practice requires a full-time commitment even if your practice is only part-time. Next time someone asks you what you do, think about their perception of your answer. Next time you prepare yourself and your clients for a hearing, think about their perception of the process. Next time you answer your phone, your email, or door … think about their perception of you and your practice. If you have the right mindset to market your practice – the sky is the limit of success.

There are seven primary components to this workbook. Using the blank spaces on each page answer the questions to the best of your ability. If you have any questions, concerns, or need more information please don't hesitate to contact me at Natalie@HowToMarketMyMediationPractice.com. And for more information, resources, and articles, follow my blog at www.HowToMarketMyMediationPractice.com

1. YOUR MARKETING MESSAGE

First things first. In order to begin a marketing campaign you need to have a marketing message. That is… an understanding of you, your service, and your clients' needs. Carefully consider the following questions and use the space provided to note your thoughts. You'll use these notes in following pages.

A. You: What is your background or specialty?

B. Service: What solution do you provide? What kind of practice do you have/want?

C. Competition: who are your competitors?

D. Differentiation: what makes you stand apart from your competitors?

E. Clients: What people or industry do you serve and where are they?

F. Needs: What are the needs of the clients you serve?

G. Benefits: what are the core benefits a client receives from your service?   .

2. DETERMINING YOUR TARGET MARKET

The more specific you are about who your target market is, the easier it will be for you to speak to them and write for them as well as what to offer them and how to find them. If your background is in architecture for instance, you should consider your target market to be construction attorneys, architects, engineers, general contractors, etc.

1. Demographics – what kind of industry (its size, location, licensing practice etc.) or individuals (perhaps situation, income, gender, education, etc.) will you specialize in?

2. Psychographics – what values, philosophy, interests, or characteristics best describe your clients?

3. Challenges – what are your target market's predicaments?

4. Points of Contact – where can you find these companies / people? What do they read, where do they network, and what media are they tuned in to? Who are the gatekeepers?

3. HOW TO WRITE AN EXECUTIVE SUMMARY

Every business needs some kind of written material or internet collateral to communicate what they offer and the advantages of doing business with them. An executive summary is the first page of your brochure or web site. It should communicate the essence of what your offer.

1. Solution statement – simple phrase that communicates the essence of your solution.

"I help conflict resolution providers develop their practice".

Write your solution statement here:

2. Problem – discuss the predicament faced by the majority of your target market to make it clear that you both understand the problem and you understand their industry.

"One of biggest challenges for ADR providers is finding the time to promote themselves and knowing how to go about an effective promotion"

 www.HowToMarketMyMediationPractice.com

3. Solution – discuss what's possible if you solve this problem.

"My clients are able to concentrate on providing the services at which they excel without having to worry about marketing and promoting their practice".

4. Why – discuss why companies are stuck in #1 and #2.

"Highly competent professionals are frequently sole-proprietors who, though very competent practitioners, have little or no background in marketing".

5. What you need to do – discuss the steps necessary to resolve this issue.

"The best investment a resolution professional can make is in increasing their visibility and establishing themselves as an authority through effective marketing and promoting."

6. Why us? At statement of why you are qualified to provide the above solution.

"I've spent more than two decades helping clients worldwide build thriving practices".

4. OUTLINE FOR EITHER PRINT COLLATERAL OR WEB SITE CONTENT

This outline can be used for any written materials or for a web site. Your aim is to communicate the advantages of your service. The key is to be clear, concise and complete in outlining what you do and the benefits that you offer.

The keys to communication are clarity and brevity.

1. Executive summary – one page outlining the essence of your services.

2. Need help? This page goes into more depth about the problem/ predicament /pain. It lets the client know whether they have the kind of issue you can help them with or not.

3. Services – this page gives an overview of the various services you offer and the advantages and benefits of those services.

4. Clients – this page provides a list of clients you've worked with, testimonial quotes and case studies of various successful projects.

5. How we work – this page outlines the process of working with your company. What you do, how you do it

6. About us – this page contains background material on the company and principal(s) of your company, including philosophy, values and approach to client work

7. Articles / Blog – published or unpublished articles on areas related to your field of expertise.

8. Resources – Any other relevant material that would be of interest to a client – links to other web sites, a book list, questionnaire, etc.

9. FAQ Page – Frequently answered questions are often useful in summarizing what you do and the benefits you offer.

10. Contact us – what they need to do to be in touch with you and how you start working with clients.

5. Creating The Ultimate Elevator Pitch

When someone asks you what you do, what do you say?

Below are some guidelines for creating an attention-getting elevator pitch.

Picture this: You're at a holiday party on the 8th floor of a local hotel. As you step into the elevator at the end of the evening the person standing next to you casually asks,

"So, what do you do"?

You have 8 floors and perhaps thirty seconds to give them an explanation that they can understand, that intrigues them, that makes them remember you (favorably) and that will entice them to contact you for further information.

It's not as hard as it sounds.

Some of the key ingredients for an effective elevator pitch are:
• Clarity
• Brevity
• Connotatively positive words
• Action verbs &
• Confidence

First, your elevator pitch must be a clear enough message that the listener doesn't need a dictionary to understand your statement. If your pitch creates more confusion than clarity then it's headed in the wrong direction. You may have to create two versions of your pitch if your practice specialty is highly technical. For instance if your specialty is hearing information technology disputes and you happen to be attending an information technology conference, then your pitch can most likely be very technical in nature and not create any confusion on the part of the listener. However, if you are attending a party for the local Chamber of Commerce and are riding with someone who is not a member of the information technology industry, then you will probably lose them with the high tech version. In this scenario you want to use "kitchen English" the form of English that most folks use around their kitchen table. Be careful that you don't talk down to your listener – the goal is to attract them as a client or base of referrals, not to insult their intelligence.

Second, you must keep your pitch brief. Remember, you've only got 8 floors (unless you're from my home town in which case you'd only have 2 floors) and just seconds to relay the specialization of your practice, your target market and the benefits that market receives from your service. In a perfect world you want to create a definition of what you do that is no longer than a single (short) sentence. For many arbitrators and mediators however, their specialty will require two or perhaps three sentences. Keep in mind that if your pitch is too long – you'll lose the listener in your monologue.

Next, and very importantly, you must convey your pitch using the most positively charged words at your disposal. I know, I know, that sounds nearly impossible for an industry that is seemly about conflict and disputes.

But is it really?

Isn't our industry more about resolution, peace, communication, closure, teamwork, hope, building relationships, solutions and much more? In fact yes. We specialize in communicating, facilitating and conciliating, not conflict and disputes. This is an important distinction not just for the mindset of providers but very important to our clients. Because what they're buying is the prospect of hope, peace of mind, restful nights, etc. They are not in the market for a dispute, they already have that – what they want to purchase is a solution. Make your pitch about the solution and you've sold them.

Another aspect of your pitch is what your English teachers always wanted of you – "Active Voice". Choose those words that are strong not weak (for example -. a. I specialize in working with mediators or b. I work with mediators). Notice the difference in power between working and work? Keep it strong – keep it active.

And finally, say it with confidence. Insertions of "uummm" and "well ahh" tell the listener that you are not too sure what you provide, for whom, or to what level of quality. To overcome this very common mistake simply write down your elevator pitch and practice saying it out loud over and over until it no longer sounds like a scripted monologue, but an easy conversational response to a very common question.

The goal of your elevator pitch is clearly and briefly define your practice in a memorable and simple phrase that is said with confidence. Your pitch should be just the beginning of an exchange of dialogue, contact information, and hopefully your services.

Following are 4 very simple steps to create the ultimate elevator pitch. I've written a sample of mine, what is yours?

1. State who you work with first.
"I work with conflict resolution providers…."

2. Articulate the predicament your target market most often faced by your target market in terms that are meaningful to them.

"…who need assistance marketing and promoting their practice."

3. Provide the solution or benefit to the problem you just articulated.

"I work with these resolutionists to develop strategies to attract clients."

4. Tell the listener what sets you apart from your competition.

"I have a track record of increasing my client's case load from part-time to full time in less than one year".

Six Promotional Strategies Vital for Success

1. Direct Touch – how can you best approach qualified prospects?
2. Networking– how can you gain credibility within a network?
3. Writing– how can you gain credibility by communicating your expertise?
4. Speaking– how can you stand out as an expert?
5. Social Media - what tools can you best use to stay in touch?
6. Referrals – how can you build on the network of those you already know?

1. DIRECT MARKETING TIPS AND TECHNIQUES

First on the list is direct mail marketing. Direct mail marketing is a great way to contact potential clients and alert them to your services. The best part about direct mail marketing, if it's done right, is that it will stand out against the barrage of emails, texts, and digital alerts that we all receive all day and night. The tricky part in direct mail is getting recipients to open the piece of mail. There are several ways to get your mailers opened.

Think carefully about the packaging. The more unique, more professional, more personalized the piece of mail is, the more likely your recipient is to open it out of curiosity. You should consider the size of your target market and establish a budget (don't forget to include postage). Use cardboard tubes, use priority mail, Fed-Ex, etc Essentially, use anything that you think will bring attention to your piece in such a way that it will get opened.

Use colorful stamps that are industry or time appropriate instead of a bulk mail indicia to send your print media. Make it easy for the recipient to contact you - attach a business card to every piece of mail you send.

Remember to employ the 60-30-10 rule when you campaign for new business using the direct mail tactic. Sixty percent of direct mail success lies in using the right mailing list; thirty percent depends on you making the right offer; and ten percent depends upon your creative packaging.

The more personalized your piece, the more likely you are to receive a response. For additional attention, hand-write a post-script on the piece, on a post-it-note, or on the outside of the mailer (Use a colored ink pen and traditional yellow notes so that your recipient knows that you took the time to think about them and them alone). Also, hand-addressed envelopes are opened 72% more often than computer generated addresses.

You should expect a minimal response of 0.005% and a maximum of 0.20% rate of response. If your mailer falls under the minimum, reformat it immediately. The single worst waste of money in marketing is to continue spending time and money on a promotional piece that isn't working. On the other hand, if your mailer receives higher than 0.20%, you've not only got a success on your hands but have far exceeded the expectations of any advertising agency.

When your mother told you that first impressions are the most important, she was right. This especially holds true for marketing. Consider your primary mailer and the following call an interview. Your customer is interviewing not only the service you offer, but the customer service that comes with it as well. When they call you with questions, the service and information they receive on this first contact will dictate all future business, if any.

List here a few ways in which you can reach out to your target market with direct mail brochures, letters, postcards, articles, etc. that include a call to action prompting them to respond.

1.

2.

3.

4.

5.

6.

7.

8.

9.

10.

2. Make Networking Pay Off

The next marketing touch is network. For networking to be a successful way to build your ADR practice, you need to maximize the number of viable prospects you meet and develop the kind of relationship with them that is likely to lead to business.

Networking is among the most important marketing strategies you can use to build or maintain your Alternative Dispute Resolution client base. At its most basic level, networking is the practice of meeting people and, in particular, of establishing relationships with prospective clients and those likely to refer clients to you (e.g., attorneys, psychotherapists, human resources professionals).

For networking to be an effective way to market your practice, you need to focus on the quantity and quality of professional relationships you develop.

Quantity. Networking is, in part, a numbers game. Quite simply, the more people you meet, the more likely you are to find prospects and referral sources.

Professional associations' networking events, such as, Chamber of Commerce mixers or legal association luncheons can be ideal opportunities to expand your circle of professional contacts. (Plus, the costs involved are tax deductible if you save your receipts.)

To get the highest rate of return on your investment of time, carefully choose the organizations you join and the events you attend. Specifically, select the associations and meetings where you're most likely to encounter your target market. For example, if your practice specialty is employment, you should join your local employment law association and regularly attend their get-togethers. (Keep in mind that ADR meetings are great places to find colleagues, not clients.)

When a suitable networking event presents itself, get ready to do business. Dress as you would for any business meeting, and stock your wallet with business cards.

If you are one of the many people who feel nervous during these events, chances are you talk only to people you already know or you latch onto someone and spend all your time with him or her--that is, if you don't avoid these gatherings altogether! By sticking within your comfort zone, you may squander the opportunity that these events present, however.

One way to manage networking shyness is to volunteer to serve at the meeting's sign-in table. This role provides a comfortable way to meet all of the attendees.

Whether or not you opt to work at the registration booth, you should set a goal to introduce yourself and give your business card to at least, say, five new people. Having a numeric target will help keep your focus on quantity and, therefore, maximize the effectiveness of your time.

Bear in mind that the one-time, press-the-flesh contact rarely turns into a client or referral source, however. Building a connection requires repeated interaction. When attending a networking function you should, therefore, reconnect with people you've met before in addition to initiating conversations with those you don't yet know.

Quality. For networking to be profitable, you not only need to direct your energy toward meeting a large number of the right people, you also need to attend to the quality of the relationships you establish with them. Specifically, you want to engage in the kinds of interactions with people that will lead them to hire you.

The three attributes you want to convey to prospects are your likeability, credibility, and usefulness.

Likeability. People want to give business to people they like. And people like those who are genuinely interested in them. When you meet someone at a meeting, event, or social gathering, use your ability to craft good open-ended questions and your active listening skills to find out about the person's concerns and needs.

Be careful, however, not to monopolize his or her time in an in-depth conversation. Exchange cards, and then contact the prospect via phone, personal note, or e-mail shortly afterwards. Keeping in touch with the people you meet increases the likelihood that they will become clients and referral sources.

Credibility. People also choose to do business with those they trust. Becoming an active and visible member of the professional associations you join is one of the best ways to build relationships in which you establish your credibility. Serve on a committee, lead a project, or chair a fundraising event. You'll earn the respect and trust from the other members of the work group (your target market), which is imperative to gaining their business.

Usefulness. In addition to doing business with those they like and trust, people forge professional relationships with those who fulfill one or more of their business needs. Prospective clients will be inclined to hire you if they believe that you will help solve one of their pressing problems. And prospective referral sources will direct customers your way if they are confident that you will support their business.

When establishing relationships with clients and referral sources, be mindful to "serve before you sell"--that is, give something of value to them (e.g., relevant information, helpful advice) before suggesting they do business with you. In particular, the more clients you refer to those in your professional network, the more clients they will be inclined to refer to you. Reciprocity is key to effective networking.

 www.HowToMarketMyMediationPractice.com

Networking Issues Ethics. Networking with prospective clients can raise an ethical red flag. Your neutrality (or perceived neutrality) may be compromised when mediating or arbitrating a case in which one of the parties is someone with whom you've cultivated a relationship. You need to be especially careful, therefore, to maintain an appropriate professional distance in your interactions with potential clients. By exclusively networking with referral sources (e.g. attorneys, behaviorists)--and not with prospective customers--you can avoid this thorny issue altogether.

Time Commitment. As noted above, building relationships that lead to business requires repeated interaction. Networking is, therefore, both a time-consumptive activity and a long-term marketing strategy.

Just being listed as a member of a professional association or showing up at the annual dinner won't be enough to drum up a lot of new business. The more you show up, get involved, and keep in touch with the people you meet week after week and month after month, the more likely you will garner new clients and referral sources.

Since generating new business takes time, you don't want to wait to start networking when you need business right away. So, even those lucky providers who have plenty of business at present are best advised to remain active in at least one professional organization to ensure that their client stream continues to flow steadily in the future.

10 Tips for One-On-One Networking

1. Arrive at meetings and group activities at least fifteen minutes early.
2. Stop waiting for something to happen to you – take the initiative.
3. Always speak with a smile and confidence.
4. Carry a large supply of business cards.
5. Make sure you get a business card from the people you meet.
6. Have a pen or pencil handy to make notes on the cards of your contacts for follow-up information.
7. Concentrate on the one person to whom are speaking – don't be guilty of roving eyes.
8. Stay at least fifteen minutes after the event to exchange cards.
9. Follow-up immediately with anyone who expressed an interest in your service.
10. Always send a thank-you note or place a phone call of thanks to anyone who sends you business.

Networking is probably the most powerful marketing tool available to conflict resolutionists. As with most service businesses, no one will hire you if they don't know and like you. As neutrals this puts us in a tough position. We have to get to know our potential clients and sources of referral well enough for them to trust us with their conflicts, but not so well that we would endanger the process (don't forget to disclose your relationship in both pre-hearing and hearing!).

1. Where or with whom to network – list some places and groups to network.

a) Professional associations or organizations

b) Leads groups

2. Leverage your networking – think of some ideas to leverage your networking for maximum results.

a) Participation

b) Leverage

3. Writing & Publishing

The third marketing touch is Writing and Publishing. Writing and disseminating articles, reports, white pages, blogs and books can be a very powerful way to establish yourself as an authority in your niche, create credibility, and educate your target market about the benefits of ADR to their industry.

Writing content is all about persuading and motivating your reader. In order to persuade and motivate your reader you will need to break the process of writing into two sections – the first is prior to writing and the second is while you're writing.

Prior to writing you need to analyze your service. First, analyze your practice from both your perspective and your potential client's. Find those qualities about your service that you think will be of greatest interest to your target market. Second, think about your position in the market place. How and why is your practice and service superior to the competition? Third, what are the tastes of your readers? Are they executives, teenagers, housewives, etc.? Alter the "tone" of your message depending on the personality and of the reader. And fourth, does the copy you have in mind fit with your entire marketing concept?

While you're writing it's imperative not to lose sight of the objective: to sell your service. Remember to use words that persuade and motivate. Write to sell. Following are seven things to keep in mind while writing.

1. Don't overstate with too many words like fabulous and extraordinary. They will destroy your credibility.

2. Be accurate and truthful.

3. Be specific. Vague approximations leave the reader unsatisfied.

4. Be organized. Your message should progress logically from headline to clincher.

5. Write for easy reading. The style should suit your reader, but some rules apply to all content writing. Seek to write smooth, uncluttered, involving and persuasive content.

6. Don't offend the reader. Be careful using humor.

7. Revise and edit – revise and edit – revise and edit.

If you want a brochure or website to promote your practice then there are a few guidelines to keep in mind when sitting down to begin the creative process. First you need to establish some clear goals for your media. What will the primary use be? The most common are:

• To act as a catalyst or call to action for potential clients,
• To act as a reference for your services,
• To support other marketing activities.

Most small practices or firms will employ a brochure or website which will of course need content. Make a list of what you want to convey to prospects. What service will you include? What biographical information will you provide? Do you have illustrations to use? Can you list testimonials and endorsements? These are the facts section of your brochure or web site.

Your next list should include the primary concerns and issues your readers will have about the service you offer. For instance, if your practice specializes in construction arbitration a main concern for potential clients will be whether or not you have a specific and extensive background in the construction industry. Readers want to know if you can "speak their construction language" and read their specialized reports and blueprints fluently.

Other examples of potential issues are what the costs will be, how long the process will take, is the process formal or informal, does the reader need an attorney or not, how can they engage the other party, etc. Whatever you identify as the readers' main concerns should be addressed in your content. I happen to think that a good rule of thumb for this section is that it should consume more than half of the brochure's or website's space. You want to make sure that the reader understands that your practice understands the reader.

The concerns and issues that the majority of your readers will need to have addressed should be listed in subheads that create the main copy on the inside panels. And the facts about your services and the processes you offer should be organized in the copy with their respective illustrations.

The same holds true for a web site. The opening page should contain your logo or illustration and a short, clear description of your practice and its target market. When you create your website content a rule of 90 – 10 is best. 90% of the site should be about the reader and their issues and concerns being met and managed and 10% of the site should be about you, the provider.

If you're not clear on the content or its reason for existence – the reader won't be either and you've just wasted your efforts on something that won't stand a chance at reaching its marketing goals.

1. Topics & titles – think of a topic that will do two things. Showcase your knowledge of the subject and be of interest to your readers.

2. Headline – the goal for your headline is to gain attention and drive interest.

3. Content – clarity and brevity are the keys to communication.

4. Publishing – list trade publications, newsletters, e-zines, and newspapers whose readers will be interested in reading your article.

5. Leverage – list ways in which you can use your published article to promote your practice.

The key to effectively communicating with potential clients is same key many mediators and arbitrators utilize in their practice and offer their clients as advice **… Clarity and Brevity**. Simply write what you mean in a succinct fashion. People will respond to this technique of clarity and brevity if you are tactful and truthful. Just say it!

4. Speak Up!

Number four on the list is speaking. One powerful method of marketing is public speaking. For those of you are comfortable with presenting information or educational speeches to an audience, you can easily establish yourself as an authority in your target market's industry. For those of you who barely escape getting hives at the mere thought of public speaking you might want to consider a partnership with someone who is an experienced and professional speaker. The benefits to speaking directly to your target market are multifold. You put yourself forward as an authority in both your own industry and your target markets, you can more easily create a relationship with a potential client, and you will receive invaluable feedback about your target market's goals, preferences, and aspirations in choosing a provider.

Speaking may also be in the form of training. Does your target market need continuing education credits to maintain their license or certification? If so, consider providing them a short course on the application of resolution communication, negotiation, mediation, arbitration or other form of ADR.

So speak up, speak out, and let your prospects hear and meet you. Below are some timeline tips if you're handling the promotion yourself.

> 1. Check the industry's calendar for their monthly and annual meetings. Either become involved in the association's event or schedule your own so that it does not conflict with theirs. Most organizations require six months to a year advance notice for annual conferences and a couple of weeks to a year for monthly meetings. Choose a date that is a minimum of 90 days away, but preferably in excess of 120 days.

2. Choose a date that provides you enough time to create a database or arrange for use of the association's newsletter and member database. Give this section of preparation your best timeline guess, and then double that amount of time.

3. Set aside enough time (and money) for creating your web site or print media (including any handouts) and addressing and applying postage or email campaign time. Double the expected time for creation and service to create a marketing safety net for yourself.

4. For events that require participants to travel or make overnight accommodations (especially for multiple-day events), you should give them 90 to 180 days advance notice. For events that are designed for a local group or if the event will consume a single day, four to eight weeks' notice is sufficient.

Speaking Engagements

Next to networking, speaking may be the most powerful marketing tool available for resolutionists. It gains you immediate credibility and authority. For many providers speaking is easier than networking. Networking requires you to approach your target market, whereas speaking allows those who are interested in your service to approach you.

1. Topics – choose a topic that would be of interest to your target market.

2. Titles – as with headlines, write a title that will grab attention and create interest.

3. Outline & practice – have a clear outline of your content and practice, practice, practice.

4. Booking a gig – list those associations and organizations to which your target market belongs and research their conference schedules, meeting schedules, etc.

5. Leverage – list some ways in which you can leverage your speaking (either past, present, or future) to promote your business. Remember that unless ADR providers are your target market, you want to focus outside our industry.

5. Social Media

These are just basics that you need to know about social media. The commonly used social media platforms for neutrals are LinkedIn, Twitter, Google+, and Facebook. Each of these platforms provide a profile page for you to explain who you are and what you do. A profile page is for your image and biographical information. The goal of a good profile is to get people to pay attention to your social-media activities.

According to Wordstream.com social media marketing, or SMM, is a form of internet marketing that involves creating and sharing content on social media networks in order to achieve your marketing and branding goals. Social media marketing includes activities like posting text and image updates, videos, and other content that drives audience engagement, as well as paid social media advertising.

Picking a social media screen name isn't tricky. The only thing I can recommend you avoid is getting to 'cutesy' with your screen name. If you're marketing your business, use the business name. If you're marketing yourself, use your name. In a perfect world, the screen name you choose is the same for every social media platform.

We've created this guide to provide you with an introduction to social media marketing and some starter social media marketing tips and training to improve your business's social presence.

With these tips, you can begin developing your own social media marketing expert plan.

Social Media and Marketing: Start With a Plan

Before you begin creating social media marketing campaigns, consider your business's goals. Starting a social media marketing campaign without a social strategy in mind is like wandering around a forest without a map—you might have fun, but you'll probably get lost.

Here are some questions to ask when defining your social media marketing goals:

- What are you hoping to achieve through social media marketing?

- Who is your target audience?

- Where would your target audience hang out and how would they use social media?

- What message do you want to send to your audience with social media marketing?

Your business type should inform and drive your social media marketing strategy.

For example, an e-commerce or travel business, being highly visual, can get a lot of value from a strong presence on Instagram or Pinterest. A business-to-business or marketing company might find more leverage in Twitter or Linkedin.

<u>How Social Media Marketing Can Help You Meet Your Marketing Goals</u>

Social media marketing can help with a number of goals, such as:

- Increasing website traffic
- Building conversions
- Raising brand awareness
- Creating a brand identity and positive brand association
- Improving communication and interaction with key audiences

The bigger and more engaged your audience is on social media networks, the easier it will be for you to achieve every other marketing goal on your list!

<u>Best Social Media Marketing Tips</u>

Ready to get started with marketing on social media? Here are a few social media marketing tips to kick off your social media campaigns.

- **Social Media Content Planning** — As discussed previously, building a social media marketing plan is essential. Consider keyword research and competitive research to help brainstorm content ideas that will interest your target audience. What are other businesses in your industry doing to drive engagement on social media?
- **Great Social Content** — Consistent with other areas of online marketing, content reigns supreme when it comes to social media marketing. Make sure you post regularly and offer truly valuable information that your ideal customers will find helpful and interesting. The content that you share on your social networks can include social media images, videos, infographics, how-to guides and more.
- **A Consistent Brand Image** — Using social media for marketing enables your business to project your brand image across a variety of different social media platforms. While each platform has its own unique environment and voice, your business's core identity, whether it's friendly, fun, or trustworthy, should stay consistent.
- **Social Media for Content Promotion** — Social media marketing is a perfect channel for sharing your best site and blog content with readers. Once you build a loyal following on social media, you'll be able to post all your new content and make sure your readers can find new stuff right away. Plus, great blog content will help you build more followers. It's a surprising way that content marketing and social media marketing benefit each other.
- **Sharing Curated Links** — While using social media for marketing is a great way to leverage your own unique, original content to gain followers, fans, and devotees, it's also an opportunity to link to outside articles as well. If other sources provide great, valuable information you think your target audience will enjoy, don't be shy about linking to them. Curating and linking to outside sources improves trust and reliability, and you may even get some links in return.
- **Tracking Competitors** — It's always important to keep an eye on competitors— they can provide valuable data for keyword research and other social media marketing insight. If your competitors are using a certain social media marketing

channel or technique that seems to be working for them, considering doing the same thing, but do it better!

- **Measuring Success with Analytics** — You can't determine the success of your social media marketing strategies without tracking data. Google Analytics can be used as a great social media marketing tool that will help you measure your most triumphant social media marketing techniques, as well as determine which strategies are better off abandoned. Attach tracking tags to your social media marketing campaigns so that you can properly monitor them. And be sure to use the analytics within each social platform for even more insight into which of your social content is performing best with your audience.
- **Social Media Crisis Management** — Things don't always go swimmingly for brands on social media. It's best to have a playbook in place so your employees know how to handle a snafu. Check out our guide to social media crisis management to see examples of the worst social media disasters, plus tips on how they *should* have been handled.

How to Choose the Best Social Media Platforms for Marketing

Here's a brief overview about how to use social media for marketing according to each platform's unique user base and environment. Different social media marketing sites require different approaches, so develop a unique strategy tailored for each platform.

Using Facebook for Social Media Marketing

Facebook's casual, friendly environment requires an active strategy. Start by creating a Facebook Business Fan Page. You will want to pay careful attention to layout, as the visual component is a key aspect of the Facebook experience.

Facebook is a place people go to relax and chat with friends, so keep your tone light and friendly. And remember, organic reach on Facebook can be extremely limited, so consider a cost-effective Facebook ad strategy, which can have a big impact on your organic Facebook presence as well!

Using Google+ for Social Media Marketing

Google+ entered the scene as a Facebook competitor, but it now serves a more niche audience. It won't work for everybody, but some communities are very active on Google+.

On Google+ you can upload and share photos, videos, links, and view all your +1s. Also take advantage of Google+ circles, which allow you to segment your followers into smaller groups, enabling you to share information with some followers while barring others. For example, you might try creating a "super-fan" circle, and share special discounts and exclusive offers only with that group.

You can also try hosting video conferences with Hangouts and experiment using the Hangout feature in some fun, creative ways. Some social media marketing ideas: if you're a salon, host a how-to session on how to braid your hair. If you own a local bookstore, try offering author video chats. If you're feeling adventurous, invite your +1s to your

Google+ Community. Google+ Communities will allow you to listen into your fan's feedback and input, truly putting the social back into social media.

Using Pinterest for Social Media Marketing

Pinterest is one of the fastest growing social media marketing trends. Pinterest's image-centered platform is ideal for retail, but anyone can benefit from using Pinterest for social media purposes or sales-driving ads.

Pinterest allows businesses to showcase their product offerings while also developing brand personality with eye-catching, unique pinboards. When developing your Pinterest strategy, remember that the social network's primary audience is female. If that's your demographic, you need a presence on Pinterest!

Using Twitter for Social Media Marketing

Twitter is the social media marketing tool that lets you broadcast your updates across the web. Follow tweeters in your industry or related fields, and you should gain a steady stream of followers in return.

Mix up your official tweets about specials, discounts, and news with fun, brand-building tweets. Be sure to retweet when a customer has something nice to say about you, and don't forget to answer people's questions when possible. Using Twitter as a social media marketing tool revolves around dialog and communication, so be sure to interact as much as possible to nurture and build your following.

Using LinkedIn for Social Media Marketing

LinkedIn is one of the more professional social media marketing sites. LinkedIn Groups is a great venue for entering into a professional dialog with people in similar industries and provides a place to share content with like-minded individuals. It's also great for posting jobs and general employee networking.

Encourage customers or clients to give your business a recommendation on your LinkedIn profile. Recommendations makes your business appear more credible and reliable for new customers. Also browse the Questions section of LinkedIn; providing answers helps you get established as a thought leader and earns trust.

Using YouTube for Social Media Marketing

YouTube is the number one place for creating and sharing video content, and it can also be an incredibly powerful social media marketing tool. Many businesses try to create video content with the aim of having their video "go viral," but in reality those chances are pretty slim. Instead, focus on creating useful, instructive "how-to" videos. These how-to videos also have the added benefit of ranking on the video search results of Google, so don't under-estimate the power of video content!

Signing Off

Every day your company sends emails, usually with empty space after your salutation and signature just begging to be used. So why not make this space work twice as hard for you? Redesign your signature to include news about your company for customers and contacts. Most importantly of course is provide current and easy to use contact information. Are you on LinkedIn? Insert the hyperlink that when clicked leads people directly to your bio page.

Track it Down

Secrets of the Spreadsheet – instead on spending more money on your marketing, stop and analyze the money you're currently spending. Create a simple spreadsheet that can track the rates of response to website or blog click throughs, referrals, direct mail or email, networking efforts etc. By tracking the rates of response to each promotional effort you'll be able to determine where your marketing is paying off (or not). If you can't measure your marketing, you have to questions if it's worth doing."

> *"She's dynamic!"*   Mediator / Tax Attorney
>
> *"Fabulous! Clear, informative, & energetic!"*   Counselor / Mediator
>
> *"I loved the specifics – both the do's and the don'ts!"*   Mediator / Labor law attorney
>
> *"Very dynamic and instructive. Natalie kept it fun and interesting"* Employment attorney / Mediator
>
> *"Best money I've spent in 35 years of practice!"*   Civil Litigator / Mediator
>
> ***"Excellent! – her presentation skills are super! I found ALL the information helpful and well organized. She has a great sense of humor!"***   University Professor and Ombudsman
>
> *"I will recommend her to everyone! She's the best instructor I've ever had!"*
> Mediator / Attorney / Marriage and Family Therapist

6. Referrals and Testimonials

Those seemingly magic referrals. They come from both satisfied clients who have first-hand knowledge about you and the services you offer, and from your marketing message. There are six key ways in which you can encourage referrals

1. Performance – How can you provide exceptional customer service while also providing your usual high-quality service?

3. Marketing message – how can you communicate in a clear and brief manner what your service or solution is?

4. Ask – It might be as simple as just asking for a referral or testimonial. Think about how and when asking will be appropriate for your satisfied clients.

5. Strategic alliances – list some of the businesses in your geographic target area that offer a non-competitive, but complimentary service to joint venture with.

6. Surveys – create a short survey about your service (SurveyMonkey.com is a great resource for this) and ask them about their experience with you. Ask them how likely they are to refer business to you. This will let them know that you actively seek referrals. Be sure to leave one open-ended question that will lead them to give you a testimonial.

Trust. It's why people hire you. But it takes a lot of time and money to persuade a prospect to trust you enough to give you his business. The best way to generate trust is obvious but it isn't used very much – Testimonials. That's why I recommend using testimonials at every opportunity. They're free, relatively easy to get, and flexible enough to add potency to almost any marketing campaign. Best of all they're believed.

The primary reason that people don't buy from you is not price, location, or service (though to continue in business for any length of time these elements must be present in spades). No, it's usually trust. People are afraid of spending too much, of buying a lousy service, of not getting the service they need. Trust is the critical element in closing the sale. That's where testimonials can be put into action. Prospective clients are far more likely to trust what others have to say about your service than what you have to say about yourself.

It's easy to do. Testimonials can be compiled by sending out a simple survey in which you ask your clients to rate your service, speed, cost, etc. Invite them to make comments on their letterhead, letting them know that their comments will be used in your marketing.

Once you have one testimonial or hundred put them to work for you.

* Print a booklet of your best testimonials (the thicker the better) and send them to your customers, to prospects, and to the media.

* Use testimonials in your print ads.

* Devote at least one panel in your brochure to testimonials from customers.

* Put testimonials on the walls of your conference or meeting area, or on a wall where your customers can see them.

PLAN – PLAN - PLAN

Pilots file a flight plan - Architects draw blueprints prior to constructing a building – Generals create battle plans – and successful businesses utilize marketing plans, business plans, and communication plans. The last pages of this workbook have a marketing plan for you to fill out.

Marketing plans do not need to be lengthy, complicated documents that require a decoder ring to understand. Most ADR practices are small firms or sole proprietors that need a marketing plan that is simple and inexpensive to implement. Below are the bare necessities for a marketing plan. For expansion on these points call our offices and we'll help you define them as they pertain to your individual practice. Following is a simple marketing plan that has been designed with conflict resolution providers in mind.

Seven Critical Elements of Your Marketing Plan

1. The benefit to consumers
2. Your positioning in the marketplace: What business are you in?
3. Your target market
4. Your advertising strategy and positioning
5. Your budget
6. The tools and techniques you'll use to reach your audience
7. A month-by-month implementation timetable

The marketing plan is a problem-solving document. Skilled problem solvers recognize that a big problem is usually the combination of several smaller problems. The best approach is to solve each of the smaller problems first, thereby dividing the big problem into manageable pieces. Your marketing plan should take the same approach. It should be a guide on which to base decisions and should ensure that everyone in your organization is working together to achieve the same goals. A good marketing plan can prevent your organization from reacting to problems in a piecemeal manner and even help in anticipating problems. Following are some guidelines to help you develop a marketing plan to support the strategy you have selected for your practice.

MARKETING PLAN WORKSHEET

This is the marketing plan of _____

I. MARKET ANALYSIS
A. Target Market - Who are the primary, secondary, and tertiary target markets?
  1. We will be selling to

  2. We will be targeting customers by which geographic area?

B. Competition
  1. Who are our competitors?
  Name _____
  Address _____
  Years in Business _____
  Market Share _____
  Price/Strategy _____
  Service _____
  Features _____
  Name _____
  Address _____
  Years in Business _____
  Market Share _____
  Price/Strategy _____
  Service _____
  Features _____

  2. How competitive is the market?
  High _____
  Medium _____
  Low _____

3. List below your strengths and weaknesses compared to your competition (consider such areas as location, size of resources, reputation, services, personnel, etc.):

Strengths   Weaknesses
1._____   1._____
2._____   2._____
3._____   3._____
4._____   4._____

II. SERVICE ANALYSIS

    A. Description

        1. Describe here what the specifically your service is and what it does:

    B. Comparison

        1. What advantages does our service have over those of the competition (consider such things as unique features, expertise, special training, etc.)?

        2. What disadvantages does it have?

III. MARKETING STRATEGIES

    A. Image, what kind of image do we want to have (such as cheap but good, or exclusiveness, or customer-oriented or highest quality, or convenience, or speed, or ...)?

B. Features - List the features we will emphasize:

C. Pricing
    1. We will be using the following pricing strategy:
        a. Suggested price _____
        b. Competitive _____
        c. Below competition _____
        d. Premium price _____
        e. Other _____

    2. Are our prices in line with our image?
        YES ___ NO ___

    3. Do our prices cover costs and leave a margin of profit?
        YES ___ NO ___

D. Customer Services
    1. List the customer services we provide:

    2. These are our sales/credit terms:

    3. The competition offers the following services:

    www.HowToMarketMyMediationPractice.com

E. Advertising/Promotion
    1. These are the things we wish to say about the business:

    2. We will use the following advertising/promotion sources:

- ☐ Radio
- ☐ Television
- ☐ Direct mail
- ☐ Personal contacts
- ☐ Trade associations
- ☐ Newspaper
- ☐ Magazines
- ☐ Email
- ☐ Billboard
- ☐ Social media
- ☐ Other

3. The following are the reasons why we consider the media we have chosen to be the most effective:

One last bit of advice: My most successful clients are those who understand that they are first and foremost a business person – an entrepreneur. They just happen to specialize in the resolution industry. These clients read business and marketing books and attend business and marketing seminars regularly. They would be successful entrepreneurs in nearly any service industry into which I could drop them. Being a great mediator or arbitrator isn't enough. Success is a multi-faceted and always evolving end.

If you have comments or questions about any of the material in this workbook, or would like some assistance in completing it, please don't hesitate to contact me at any time. I'd love to hear about your challenges and particularly your successes.

Natalie J. Armstrong-Motin
Natalie@HowToMarketMyMediationPractice.com
www.HowToMarketMyMediationPractice.com